MW00912593

and Baby makes three
the new family's first year

Parent-Tested Tips for New Moms and Dads
by Jeanne Murphy

SOURCEBOOKS, INC.
NAPERVILLE, ILLINOIS

Published by Sourcebooks, Inc.
P.O. Box 4410, Naperville, Illinois 60567-4410
(630) 961-3900
FAX: (630) 961-2168
www.sourcebooks.com

Originally published in 2000 by Fisher Books.

Library of Congress Cataloging-in-Publication Data

Murphy, Jeanne.
  And Baby Makes Three / Jeanne Murphy
    p. cm.
  ISBN 1-4022-0540-6 (alk. paper)
  1. Infants--Care--Popular works. 2. Parenting--Popular works. I. Title.

RJ61.M7997 2005
649'.122--dc22

                                    2005016464

Printed and bound in the United States of America
IN 10 9 8 7 6 5 4 3 2 1

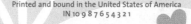

This book is dedicated to my lifelong, one and only love, my husband, Jan—the man whom each day I admire, understand, respect, and love more and more.

All love & peace,
—Jeanne

Contents

Introduction

Congratulations on the birth of your baby! Parenting is the most rewarding experience and I'm sure you'll be great at it.

You will probably find parenting easy, because adjusting to your baby is nothing compared to the changes you and your partner will experience. Here are some tested thoughts and helpful suggestions. Most importantly, stick together! Use humor whenever you start to feel tense. Smiling releases hormones that can dramatically reduce stress, and I hope this book helps in that department.

God bless you and best wishes to you and your new family.

—Jeanne

"First Comes Love..."

Use this special time in your life to renew your commitment to respect and honor each other, especially now as parents, since you'll be setting the example for your baby. Remember that sometimes in life you have to back up in order to go forward, so here are some gentle reminders and words of wisdom.

*P*ractice what you preach, especially for the sake of the baby.

*R*espect each other's wishes, especially if it pertains to the baby.

*H*ave a code to work together and never give up.

———

*D*rop your armor *first* and let go of any and all anger towards each other.

$\mathcal{I}$t's never really 50/50 between you and your partner. It's 100/100.

$\mathcal{A}$lbert Schweitzer said, "Example is not the main thing in influencing others. It's the *only* thing."

Give credit when credit is due.

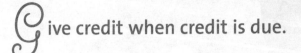

Keep all family business in your own family.

When in doubt, sleep on it.

Say what you mean and mean what you say. And by the way, you're going to need to practice this a *whole* lot for the years ahead as a parent.

Laugh at yourself.

Listen to each other everyday and try not to interrupt.

Trust and believe in each other.

Agree that you can disagree. This is the key to a long-lasting life together—especially after you become a family.

Write your feelings down and feel free to express everything on your mind. If, at the end, you see more than five sentences and it's not a romantic poem or love song, throw it away and start over...

Go the extra mile for each other—and for the baby.

Have a family dinner together every night.

Be aware of each other's feelings.

10

Believe in unity and a higher power...God.

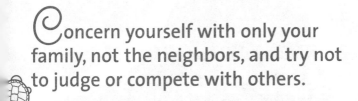

Concern yourself with only your family, not the neighbors, and try not to judge or compete with others.

$\mathcal{S}$et obtainable standards and live by them. With this, you will have surpassed them when it's all said and done.

$\mathcal{F}$orgive each other from the heart. And remember that forgiveness is the hardest thing to do, but it's also the best thing to do.

Don't go to bed mad at each other.

Make it your family ethic never to talk about your partner or your baby to another person in a negative manner.

Focus on the positive. Only share stories about your family and your adjustment to parenthood that are in a good light.

Tell your partner about everything you're thinking *first*, especially when it relates to your child.

Smile at each other and be thankful.

Take a baby-step approach to your new family and savor every minute with your partner and new child. It's so rewarding.

*P*rotect and defend each other and your family.

*A*lways respond to your partner and baby with gentleness, consideration, support, and love. Remember, saying "I love you" is the most important and special thing you can do, so say it every chance you get.

Chapter Two

Welcome to the World of Parenting

I had this vision in my mind that I would come home from the hospital with the baby smiling at my side, with time to take a walk in the stroller with my husband under a true blue sky and warm sun.

But the fact is that our baby was more than two weeks early, I didn't get one single day off work to myself, and then my boss started calling and emailing me at home with questions. I actually had to return two business phone calls from my hospital bed at 9:30 in the morning after a 5:00 a.m. delivery! I still can't believe that!

Anyway, since then for us, it's been go-go-go and there's so much to know. That's why I think you have to look out for each other and be completely considerate. Things are going to move faster now as a family, and you need to be able to count on each other completely.

Ideally, you want to go from being a husband-and-wife, to being a mom/wife-and-husband/father.

Babies bring you and your partner closer together—now, always, and forever.

Babies simply don't follow rules of society. Expect them to do things like cry, and not to stop even if you ask.

It's okay to admit that you may be a little fearful of the future. *You should be...* (Just kidding. All right, already, lighten up. This is just the beginning of the chapter.)

Getting adjusted to parenthood can be tough and it is not always a fun and happy experience, so just don't expect it to be perfect.

Stay in the loop together. If you start to feel out of it, spend quality time together *without* the baby.

Sometimes your partner's role model may not be quite what you were hoping for. You'll get what I mean as it comes out in your partner as a new parent because you tend to repeat history and act the way your parents treated you. Be patient and remember both of you can learn new things and change, so simply try to be a better role model everyday for your child.

Try not to talk *only* about the baby when you're alone together.

And since most parents are guided by what they learned from their own parents, expect your techniques to be different and try to honor them as much as you can. In fact, you can really pull your family together by complimenting each other's rituals and by letting the in-laws know how much you appreciate some of their more positive ideas.

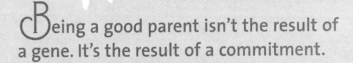

Being a good parent isn't the result of a gene. It's the result of a commitment.

23

Stress reducer tip 101: keep things organized. For instance, store thermometers, pacifiers, bibs, and diapers where they belong. I know, it's so much easier said than done but it's worth reminding you about because it's these things that make a world of difference around the house.

Love your family because you'll learn over time, they are the ones you can always and truly rely on.

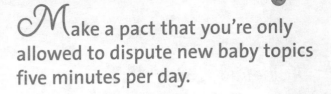

$\mathcal{M}$ake a pact that you're only allowed to dispute new baby topics five minutes per day.

$\mathcal{T}$ake up lessons and classes as a couple and try to do things together for fun. Some great ideas include tennis, bowling, golf, biking, etc. And from experience, don't wallpaper together, and I wouldn't recommend snow-skiing either. You can't risk being out of commission at the same time...for at least a few years.

Consider not going to a party or family gathering if you are tired or in a bad mood. It is not only okay, but it may be the best thing to do.

If ever you're perplexed, use a lifeline and simply call another parent. More than likely, they'll know the answer.

Find a humorous way for ending your five-minute daily baby challenge. Example, give a high five and congratulate your partner for presenting a fine case—even if this issue is not resolved.

___

If you have anything to say about the baby, but the baby is okay, consider keeping it to yourself. You might just be better off in the long run.

But, if you have something important to say that's really observant, obvious, inobvious, and/or truly helpful, absolutely speak up! Just don't say it to the baby hoping your partner will overhear it, because that drives everyone nuts.

Speak your mind on matters you have experience in.

The moment that everyone in the family agrees that the baby comes first—even for just awhile—is the moment things start to get back to normal. Now, read this tip again.

Remind each other to stop and smell the roses, because this is really a very short, special time in your life together. Okay, maybe it's *not* short, but it *is* special.

The truth of the matter is that it's all in the perspective. Happiness is found when each of the spouses feels and truly believes the load is equally carried. Carry your load.

Keep the anticipation of the new baby feeling in your family after the baby is born, and add in a "Nothing's going to stop us now" attitude.

You may start to notice how much more in agreement you are with your partner when you use baby-sitters who are not related to either one of you.

All of a sudden, it will dawn on you that the people shown in the parenting magazine photos are paid actors and models. At that point, you can drop the "new parents" title because you will have been promoted to "parents."

Getting a good night sleep affects everyone in the family, so alternate with your partner if either of you is not getting enough.

If you think you can't win, you're right. (But just for now.)

Some new parents are totally natural and easygoing with new babies and some are just not. Be patient and guess what? Babies will usually teach the ones who are not natural how to handle them at an early age if they feel love. Babies love those who they feel love them.

The expression "afternoon delight" now means husband comes home during his lunch hour to look after baby while wife takes a nap, or vice versa.

The instant your child is born, your perspective on life changes completely. Things you never thought much about before—like Father's Day and Mother's Day—take on a new meaning.

There's a sense of peace in having a family. Isn't there? I mean, is there? No, that's right, I mean, isn't there? Right? (ha ha)

All right, I'll admit it...the baby can cause a little jealousy in the family at first. Even the family dog can exhibit a slight change in behavior because it envies the attention on the baby.

If you ever feel like hitting something, *please* use a punching bag; and if you miss the bag and hit the wall by accident, don't worry. Most stores carry a wide variety of wall-repair kits and they're usually located in the new parenting aisle. *I'm serious.*

It's said the more you give, the more you get back. And that's just the plain truth once you become a parent.

If your baby doesn't look like either one of you at first, don't be alarmed. It's just a matter of time before the signs start to emerge. They usually show up first in the eyes, the eyebrows, and the smile. It's so beautiful. Then according to my orthodontist, they show up again later in the positioning of the teeth... and *that's* usually a scary and an expensive realization.

Use the words "I" and "we" instead of "you" whenever you can. This simple action conveys a higher level of respect to your partner, and that's what will keep you both a team. Example: "*You* should take out the garbage because the diapers smell." should be replaced with "*I* will take out the garage, because the diapers smell." See what I mean? It just kind of lands better for everyone in the family even if it doesn't sound exactly right to you at first.

There's going to be a moment when you recognize your own worst habits shine through in your child. And I must say, it is a very humbling experience.

In one day, you've gone from being a child to a being a parent. And as profound as that is, you'll also need to consider giving your parents a chance to catch up with you and that idea...

Chapter Three

Between You and Me, Dad

Congratulations, Dad!

I'm so happy for you. You are entering into a period of time that will impact you the rest of your life. This is when your character will be shining through like the sun to your wife and those around you, so use this period to prove how important fathering and family is to you.

Now is the time to think only of your wife, the new mom, and the baby. She's really experiencing some profound changes. Be patient, supportive, offer kind words and important advice, and know that the answer to the question that has baffled men for centuries is simple...

What do women want? Hmm...to be a happy family.

So here's an example of how blurring this first year can be for a new mom. For me, it was really, really blurry. That's why I wrote these books. Anyway, I remember depending on a ritual every morning, afternoon, and evening. I would microwave some water to make a cup of instant coffee or soothing tea. Then one day, in the very beginning, when we just got home from the hospital, *and* when I needed my coffee the most, my microwave died and we couldn't

afford another one—even if I had time to shop. I went without anything for days, dragging myself around in a fog with the baby. Finally, my mother called me and said, "Why don't you just boil a cup of water on the stove?" And it was like my eyes were opened to a whole new world...duh! Hello!

So if your wife is in a fog, here are ways to help.

Baby the new mother now.
She really does need it.

Remove the words, "happy hour," "office party," "office gathering," or anything vaguely resembling those terms from your vocabulary.

Keep in mind, everyone *else* may be having happy hour between 5:00–7:30 p.m., but more than likely, you'll be having "cranky hour." Don't worry, it doesn't last forever.

Don't be a better "mother" than the mother, even if you are.

Be the kind voice for your partner as it relates to things like visitors. If your partner can't speak up and tell family members and friends to try to call first and/or to reschedule, do it for her. People respect those who take care of their spouses and speak up for them—but be sure you say, "*We need some time alone!*" ever so gently. Especially to in-laws and to her friends.

As a warning, try not to use the expression, "I'm so tired" around the new mother, especially not the day after the baby is born.

As far as romance goes, give it time. She'll probably surprise you when she's ready...and at that point, you may have no idea what you're in for.

———

Notice that whenever you see a happy family, the husband is pushing the stroller, carrying the diaper bag, emptying the necessities from the car, ordering the pictures online, sending all those thank-you cards, etc., etc., etc. (hint, hint).

I keep bringing up letting mom sleep because I *can't* emphasize *enough* how important it is. Let new mom sleep whenever she can.

*K*eep in mind that even if you're working overtime to help out with the new bills, being gone a lot can make a new mom feel lonely and overburdened. There's really not a good answer for this one. You'll have to use your judgment and I'll just stay out of your family business.

If you work a long day, it's likely that the baby will be sleeping a lot of the time when you are finally home. Don't worry. You're not really missing baby's life. This will change as baby grows and she will be awake for you to enjoy very soon. In the first couple of months, all you are missing is the work behind the scenes. In fact, I think you are *so* lucky.

Golden Rule #1: Nap, but *only* when the baby naps.

$\mathcal{A}$ny and all efforts on your part will be noticed and deeply appreciated.

$\mathcal{U}$nless the new mom has an *exceptional* sense of humor, don't laugh at her while she is trying on lingerie. Getting back to prebaby weight, or somewhere in-between takes time...for both of you. It's common for new dads to put on weight during this time too, so just enjoy this period of time and laugh about it together.

Do things that you used to do together again as soon as possible... Reminder: play cards, dance, use game boards, etc. My grandparents had an ongoing gin rummy game that lasted for over twenty years.

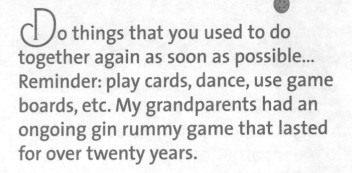

Remind the new mom to take care of herself, take vitamins, and drink lots of orange juice. This will also help if her hair has been thinning out or looks dull after having a baby. This is normal.

If the new mom shares something that is bothering her and asks you how you feel about it, agree with her in a sympathetic way, at least for the moment.

You probably know your wife's limitations more than she does, so don't let her take on more than she can handle. Be the coach of your team!

And if you don't think you know your wife's limitations, observe her. You'll probably notice a pattern when she's about to overdo it. Perhaps it's like mine, which goes like this:

1. Morning: happiness, joy, radiance
2. Noon: tension, shortness, abruptness
3. Evening: strife, screaming, crying loudly—with or without the baby. In short, a full-blown mom overload.

If this happens, especially on a regular basis, she's simply doing too much and you might want to intervene and take over by doing some extra chores or hiring some extra help.

Another important thought on that one is that stress usually only comes on when things are crazy— like the first days home from the hospital, guest visits, holidays, etc.

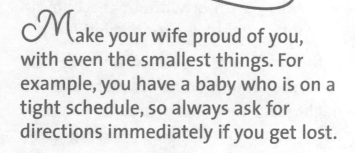

Make your wife proud of you, with even the smallest things. For example, you have a baby who is on a tight schedule, so always ask for directions immediately if you get lost.

Do yourself a favor and don't take on any new or unnecessary project. For instance, putting in a second bathroom during the first six months with a new baby may not be such a great idea. Wait on the project and put your energy into keeping things as manageable as possible. It will pay off a thousand-fold later. If, however, there are unfinished jobs, try to help finish them up to relieve some of the anxiety that things like that can cause.

As a warning, I wouldn't take up golf lessons or start any other new hobby *by yourself*, right now. Think of it like this: God just gave you a new hobby.

If your wife says she feels fat, remind her that she just had a baby. That's *so* much more important.

*I*t's true: your wife does have some of the same characteristics as a crazy person during the first few weeks postpartum. But it's only *temporary* insanity.

*H*eads-up: saying things like, "How do you know when a diaper needs to be changed?" could leave you looking silly.

Be in charge of organizing the family picture each year. You'll be so happy you did.

It's important to know that not having any company and being lonely can be just as bad as having too much and being worn out.

My father has five children and he tells me to tell you this, "Sometimes it's better to punt on the third down... especially when your wife is a new mother." He said all men would know what he means. And good thing, because I have absolutely no idea what he's talking about (and I hope he didn't ruin my book).

I say it's just easier to deal with a screaming baby than a screaming mom.

Try not to answer a question with a question, especially statements like: "How should I know?" and "What do you want me to do?" Need I say more?

Under no circumstances use the expression, "So, did you do anything today?..." unless you want to be told off, because there's a good chance you might be.

On the other hand, when everything is calm and going really well, ask to take care of the baby. The new mom will say, "No thanks!" but she'll adore you forever for asking. (See, that one works, right?)

Only talk about other moms who are fat. This *is* key.

It's important to be realistic about your new lifestyle, and you'll get along fine. It's possible that the days of perfectly pressed pants and shirts may be over for awhile. And while I'm thinking of it, you might want to expect your pockets to be filled with cereal and small toys in the near future, rather than money. Just keep the peace. That's all anyone wants, right?

Don't even think of asking if you can go to a football game on Sunday if your wife delivered the baby on Saturday. Or Friday...or Thursday...etc., etc., etc.

You'll see that everything now refers to the "*before* the baby" and "*after* the baby" stage. **Example:** Before—football, football, football. After—baby, baby, baby. Okay, sure! You can add in a "*during*" stage, just be sure to blend and balance the two evenly. Good idea!

Never, never, never wake up
the baby!

Be a star and alternate pick-ups
and drop-offs with your wife if you
both use any type of child-care facility.
Think of it as your special time alone
with the baby. Those moments are the
most rewarding of all.

*I*f you find baby's mother with beads of perspiration on her forehead and she says, "It's sweat! It is caused by *hard work*, and it is spelled S-T-R-E-S-S," you are talking to a gigantic, postpartum, hot-flash hormone, not your wife... run for it!

*I*f you come home after work and her hair is wet, her face is pale, and her robe is still on, don't worry— she's not sick, she's just exhausted.

If your wife says she needs a baby-sitter, get one *immediately*...that's another tell-tale sign of an oncoming stress-overload issue.

Once your baby arrives, *your* birthday pretty much becomes a thing of the past. (Just kidding! You may actually find that your birthday is even more special now, daddy.)

Build your budget together and don't go over it when either of you are in a bad mood.

Try not to compete with each other over who's the better parent in the family. Just do the best you can. If you're both a bit "imperfect" at it, it's because that's the way it was meant to be. You're supposed to learn about this whole deal together...and whoops! Sorry, if I'm interfering...*again*.

Things you could depend on before sometimes change a bit after the baby is born...for example, if you kicked your wife's foot under the table during a party conversation *before* the baby was born, she probably would have politely changed the subject. Now that she's a mother, there's just no time for sugarcoating. So be prepared. She might surprise you with the public announcement, "Why are you kicking my foot? And what do you want anyway?" Oops! Sorry.

Use the same expression with the baby each time you see her, something like "Uh-oh!" She will begin to bond with you and look to you the way she looks to the new mother. This is usually a wonderful experience...especially for mom!

 Basically, change completely forever.

$\mathcal{R}$emember to thank your wife for having your child.

$\mathcal{A}$ccept the fact that you're not the center of attention anymore with dignity, ease, and a great sense of humor...ha ha. And then, you'll be the one adored and talked about more than ever. The world is filled with irony like this.

$\mathcal{C}$ongratulations again on being the "father of a child." To whom much is given, much is expected. You'll get what I mean later.

$\mathcal{A}$ll right, enough said. Good luck and go for it! High five!

Chapter Four

Just Between Us, New Mom

It's hard to stay sane when emotions are running wild, sleep is a memory, people call nonstop, and confusion seems to surround you every waking moment. On top of everything, you have just delivered a real baby who looks nothing like all those pictures you've seen in magazines, and you're responsible for her welfare...forever. *It is scary* and you deserve a break!

Part of the problem is that during the pregnancy months, we get to relax, we feel good from all of the prenatal vitamins, we rest, we eat well, and we learn how to focus and breathe deeply. The minute the baby comes along, however, we forget our basic training. In short, we forget to have a "focal point."

Once you get home from the hospital, your main focal point has to be, "I can do this!" To help you through this, I'd like to give you a few thoughts you can repeat to yourself anytime you feel stressed.

Focal Points for New Moms:
(Repeat to yourself in order up to one hundred times daily)

1. Smiling is contagious.
2. People don't really need eight hours of sleep a day anyway.
3. Nobody who matters or of authority is scoring my parenting skills.
4. This is fun and I am really good at this.
5. My baby is just begging me for something simple when she cries and I love to help!

My goal in this book is to look after you so you can look after yours.

$\mathcal{I}$ think that we were given big bodies as pregnant women just to prepare us for letting go of control altogether. It's like God's speaks to us and says, "Your baby is coming and you'll see that you have to let go and work 24/7, so get used it for the next nine months and then I'll bring the baby to you." And so day-by-day we learn to sacrifice and we also adjust somehow to the profound issue of vanity...

To clarify, "postpartum depression" and the "baby blues" are two different things. "Postpartum depression" is serious and unexpected, whereas the "baby blues" are natural and expected. In fact, "baby blues" usually hit a new mom around the third day after birth and last only a week or two.

"Postpartum depression" can come on several months after the baby is born and can last a long time. If you feel signs of deep depression, see a doctor because this can be helped.

Heads-up: 10–20 percent of new moms experience postpartum depression. If the case is severe, you could think of hurting the baby. Be aware and call the doctor if you notice anything like that or if you're overfatigued, can't sleep well, and/or if you're having disturbing dreams.

Some postpartum depression signs include: lack of interest in the baby, little or no appetite, tiredness, lack of interest in family, etc. Again, see the doctor if you exhibit any of these signs.

Okay, I'm not a doctor, so what do I know? All I can say is that less interest in sex for a few weeks in the beginning is normal for women. And then, all I know is that for me, *holy moly*, it all changed *so* much! Hang in there if you're wondering what's going to happen. You'll probably pleasantly surprise yourself and your partner.

And my personal acronym for PMS is "parental-mental syndrome."

Symptoms of the baby blues range from being really weepy to being overly energetic for just a few short weeks after the baby is born. As long as it wears off, what the heck, I say enjoy either problem, right? It sounds like a dream to me. Crying is great because it relieves stress, it will make you feel better, and if you're busy, you'll get so much done. Who named it the "baby blues" anyway? I think it should be named the "New Mom Bliss Stage."

On other matters, I used to get really mad when men developed symptoms of depression after having a new baby because I thought it was irritating and selfish, and I complained about it for years. I changed my mind and now I think *anyone* who has a baby can experience overwhelming emotions, especially dad and grandparents. There are two points to this tip. The first one is that others can become overwhelmed by a birth and the second one is do you see what I mean about how dramatically you can change your mind when you have a baby and there are new hormones in your system?

Being sexy doesn't have to mean being skinny. It's a feeling of confidence, contentment, and happiness. So work it!

Emotions involve feelings, not logic...for whatever that means.

Keep a cell phone handy, and take off and let dad bond with baby. The longer and more dad bonds with baby on the front end, the better.

Avoid caffeine late in the day, especially if you're breast-feeding. This could be keeping you and possibly the baby awake at night.

Being tired is usually the combination of the new responsibilities and the new emotions, more than a result of taking care of the baby.

If it seems like every time you try to lie down, the baby wakes you up and you become frustrated, be sure to eat light foods throughout the day to give you strength, and take quick showers or baths to release the tension.

Expect yourself to freak out if you mix: 1 part postpartum hormones with 2 parts champagne or red wine.

If you're feeling like you need a boost, perk yourself up by doing something special just for yourself—like have a pedicure.

I remember having an argument only four days after the baby was born. I don't remember what the fight was about, but I do remember that although I was mad, I was also secretly elated that I had lost nearly twenty-eight pounds in just four short days! In retrospect, I think the argument may have been my fault, because I don't think you can behave rationally with that type of weight loss and hormonal fluctuation. I was wrong and I probably should have apologized to my husband. Oh well...shoulda, woulda, coulda.

Try not to say "yes" when you really mean "no." For example, if someone asks you to do something during this time and you're tired, just say, "No, I can't." It's okay.

And it's not only okay to ask for help when you need it, it's important. Remember, there are only a few good mind readers in the world.

Talk to other new parents...you'll love the camaraderie. Well, maybe not always. Every parent has their own ideas, and some parents can be really strong about expressing their opinions to you. Oops, I forgot, I guess I fall into this category, too.

Use your resources and encourage your husband to have friendships with other dads, too. It's important because they will tell it to him like it is...so you don't have to. (Wink, wink.)

Some new mothers kind-of have a distorted conception of how they look because their weight fluctuation over the course of nine months was so tremendous. On top of that, it's always *so* hard to find something to wear after the baby is born. If you're experiencing this problem, wear something black and make sure whatever it is, it's too big rather than too small.

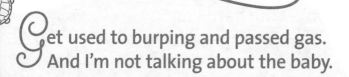

Get used to burping and passed gas. And I'm not talking about the baby.

Bear with me on this because it's a sensitive issue, but learning to be a parent really does take time and experience, so don't worry and don't try to act like you know everything about babies and being a parent the minute the baby is born. It's *sooooo* irritating! Especially to other parents and to the new dad. And I learned this—and every other tip in this book—the hard way.

$\mathcal{I}$n my opinion, women who have had children, have lived through it, and have persevered through the first year should be celebrated, loved, and adored. We are the sexiest of all creatures because we do everything to give and love unconditionally.

$\mathcal{S}$implify and enjoy your life during these years. For example, think of changing jobs to one that's closer to your home if you can.

91

Tell your husband if you do or don't want him to call you "momma" or something else *before* he picks out a new nickname for you. My nickname, which I'll keep in our family, used to grate on my nerves.

Use the library. Don't forget, it carries a wide range of books and magazines for new parents—and while you're there, why not check out a movie?

*T*think it's true, and really important to tell you too, that if you didn't need or understand any of the tips in this section, I completely envy you because you've been given a gift and you really should be proud of yourself.

My best wishes.

*A*ll of a sudden, you'll see that there's a higher level of respect that exudes from others to you when you become and say you are "a mother." It's so nice. Enjoy it—you deserve it!

Chapter Five

Baby Your Baby

The roots of a tree
    are the important part
They are the base and the place
    where its character starts.
If the roots of the tree
    are planted deep in the ground,
No matter the weather
    the tree will be sound.
                    —Jeanne Murphy, *Grassroots*

Plant the right seeds in your baby now so she will have deep and healthy roots.

During this time you or your partner may notice little things about the baby that, if shared, can make it easier for your new family. When this happens, be sure to speak up. As an example, I was frustrated trying to figure out why our son was crying during the second month. It seemed like nothing I tried was working. I tried feeding, changing the diaper, changing the scenery, etc. My husband calmly said, "He's just tired." And I was perplexed as to how *he* would know that the baby was tired, so I asked. He went on to say, "If you listen to him, you can tell by his tone what he wants. Right now, he's crying in a tired tone." I put the baby down and he was sleeping in two seconds. From that moment on, I noticed the different tones when my baby would cry and it was true, he had a bowel-movement tone, a hungry tone, etc.

Hmm. I guess my husband is right now and then after all...

Help each other by sharing and offering this information whenever you can.

*R*ocking your baby can be as soothing for you as it is for your baby.

*B*e sure to read and reread classic stories to your baby right away, like *The Three Little Pigs*. You'll be surprised at how much you'll all get out of it, like building your house out of brick instead of straw.

The first thing you give your child is your name, so make him proud of it!

Bonds between you and your baby develop over time so don't feel bad if you don't automatically have this bonding the day the baby comes home from the hospital.

Do things with the baby that you like to do and when you can enjoy the moment you're doing it. For instance, if dad is usually tired after work, have him feed the baby first thing in the morning or in the middle of the night instead.

Each baby has their own personality and you shouldn't try to change it. Love her unconditionally and enjoy her uniqueness.

*N*ever break your baby's spirit. Think always: the more challenging your baby is to you, the more fun!

*I*f anyone around your baby uses bad words, don't be surprised by his first words. My sister's first word was... well, let's move on for now. I come from a very large family and we still have a lot to cover.

Establish holiday traditions with your family. Read books such as *The Polar Express*, *'Twas the Night Before Christmas*, and *The Story of the Nativity*.

Say prayers to your infant. And remember to read *all* of the lyrics of your favorite holiday songs to your baby as he grows. They are usually prayers, and if you only say the first verse, you and your baby will probably never get the full message.

Girl or boy, you learn a lot more about people and the human body once you become a parent. Whoa...

Hold the baby in a position that *she* likes, and notice if she likes to be bounced or not—some babies just don't like being bounced at all.

If you have a special memory of your childhood, such as amusement parks, fishing, or going to the beach with your parents, make it a priority to pass the same joy down to your child and to your spouse...they'll love it, too.

Teach your child about love by loving and to sing by singing.

Remember that babies actually sleep through the night better and earlier when they have happy parents who work together and the household is calm.

If the baby is happy, leave her alone and notice if she's even happier when you do this.

The first day our second child came home from the hospital, I thought to myself, "My Lord, that child knows *exactly* what he wants." The truth is that some infants are just born intuitive, with a profound understanding of what the deal is—about everything.

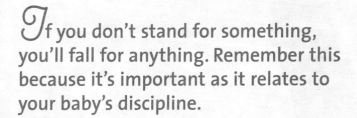

If you don't stand for something, you'll fall for anything. Remember this because it's important as it relates to your baby's discipline.

Once you become a parent, you are loved and adored in ways you never knew possible.

Chapter Six

Gifts, Romance, and All That...

I remember when our baby turned one year old. We did everything, including hire a band for the event! My husband brought in a pony from a nearby farm for the other children, who were mostly under three, while I planted flowers in the garden, cleaned like a freak, bought enough food to feed half the United States, and expected everyone to be in a glorious mood.

Well, the babies were terrified of the pony, which stressed out all of the parents. No one noticed the flowers because it ended up raining. There were all these babies crawling around everywhere in our house—except our baby, who slept through most, if not all, of the party. By 5:00 p.m., the other parents were so tired that no one stayed long enough to eat the food or hear the band. Doesn't that sound like fun? And it only cost about eight hundred dollars....ugh!

The point of that story is that doing so much is exhausting, expensive, and completely unnecessary in the first year of parenting. You'll see over time that for babies who are turning one year old, the best gift is usually an empty box. Really.

For new parents, there are a few gift ideas that I'd like to share. These are my list of the "best of the best" for either new parent. Hope you enjoy, but think always: these are the timeless gifts that will carry you not only through your first year as a parent, but your lifetime as a family.

Babies become engrossed and love things—until they can figure them out—like lids or tunnels, and then they move on to another thing that challenges them. So inexpensive gifts and the most basic and simple ones are sometimes the best.

A kiss and a hug go a long way...

I also think it's important to note that sometimes you can be as sentimental about their toys as they are. When this happens, be sure to save those special things for them for later. There is a message in everything your baby does. Learn to see it and love it, and you'll love every moment in life as a parent.

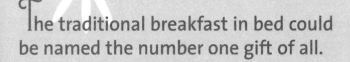

The traditional breakfast in bed could be named the number one gift of all.

$\mathcal{L}$aughter is a great gift and the best medicine. Laughter is like instant glue. It seals everything and binds it tightly together *immediately*. Comedy shows are great date ideas because they make you laugh and they take your mind completely off the baby.

$\mathcal{A}$ctions can speak louder than words.... So if you want to say, "I love you"—do the laundry.

*E*njoy a lot of take-out foods and anything that makes life easier.

*F*un, funny, and romantic *free* e-cards can be sent to your lover 24/7 via email. As a new parent, this is great! You can also send invites to a special dinner, the movies, or anything. If you're not good at gift-giving, let the pros who work for these companies do the job for you. (Ooh, it's such a perfect solution!)

115

Sleep. For example, moving the baby monitor away from mom when she falls asleep and then taking care of the baby qualifies as a present.

Tasks that take the burden off of the new mom, including things like watering the plants, organizing the gifts, and sending thank-you cards also qualify as gifts—even if it's just giving her the gift of time to let her do it herself. Kudos to you, gift giver!

Volunteer to watch your baby to let mom go shopping for anything other than groceries.

Smile. Make evenings a special time for you and your family. The first five minutes home together will set the stage and mood for the night. Make a point to smile at each other during this time.

$\mathcal{M}$ust-have: a remote-control starting device for mom's and dad's cars. It's the perfect way to warm it up or cool the car down before you get in with the baby. These devices also save you time and that—other than a back massage—is about the only thing I can think of that we all have to have nowadays.

$\mathcal{D}$on't forget a massage for mom or dad—and you can even do it yourself.

And there's always the short version, which is just as valuable— a foot massage is *the best*. Ever try it? Give your own coupon to your spouse to redeem whenever and use lots of lotion. The more the better.

Hire a baby-sitter to take the baby for a *long* walk and just relax. When he gets back, keep your sitter and then take your spouse to an afternoon movie and/or dinner.

Take two days off from work and spend a vacation at home with your new family. Just resting is rejuvenating and so needed for all of you, but don't get involved in *any* projects. I mean it—if you shut the door and a picture falls off the wall, leave it on the floor. If you shut the garage door and it breaks, save it for another day to fix it, and don't wait on the phone for an automated attendant to assist you in any manner. Make it a point to laugh when that happens, and start to follow the philosophy that those types of things will *always* happen, but your days off with your family *won't* happen—unless you make them and enjoy them.

Create a standing date and standing baby-sitter night; for example, every Friday at 7:30 p.m.

Think "low cost" when it comes to baby-sitters...they can be expensive. So plan to have a family member baby-sit half of the time you're gone, and use the baby-sitter for the second half to save money. And of course, *money* is a gift that will never go out of style.

Remember, it's the thought that counts when it comes to a gift and anything you know your partner enjoys is worth the effort.

Spend your last dollar paying someone *else* to run errands for you and your partner so you can enjoy the baby.

*H*ave your home cleaned by a professional service. Do this about a week before any family event, like the baby's first birthday party or holiday gathering for extra points.

*C*lothing or something for the parent is great. It seems that everyone focuses on gifts for the baby, but there's nothing more special than when the gift is just for the parent...the one who *really* needs pampering.

Surprise your spouse with a candlelit dinner and be sure to play the soft, familiar music that brought you two together.

And don't forget...your baby is a gift.

There are common rules in society that you should try to teach your child. In the course of considering them for this book, I noticed that they are also the rules that can keep your family happy.

- If you don't have anything nice to say, don't say anything at all.
- Put yourself in the other's shoes.
- Kiss and make up.
- Respect your elders.
- Stick together and use the buddy system.

- Take turns.
- Use the magic words with each other: "please," "thank you," "you're welcome!"
- Tell the truth.
- Be fair.
- Do good and good follows.

And don't forget the most important rule is to make your mother proud of you!

Lots of love,
—Jeanne

Index

A

adjustment to parenting, 21, 26, 30, 34, 39, 44, 45, 62, 66, 68, 84, 90, 120

advice, seeking, 88, 92

B

baby blues, 77, 80, 81

baby-sitter, 31, 66, 117, 119, 121, 122

belief, 11, 32, 102

bonding with baby, 99, 100

budget, 67

D

E

F